tales retold

poems by

Paula Bonnell

Finishing Line Press
Georgetown, Kentucky

tales retold

Copyright © 2017 by Paula Bonnell
ISBN 978-1-63534-166-9 First Edition
All rights reserved under International and Pan-American Copyright Conventions.
No part of this book may be reproduced in any manner whatsoever without written permission from the publisher, except in the case of brief quotations embodied in critical articles and reviews.

ACKNOWLEDGMENTS

My thanks to the editors of the publications in which these poems first appeared, some in slightly different form:

"Ancestral Memories" *The Andover Review*
"Chinoiserie, Before the Wars" *Manhattan Poetry Review*
"Civil War Funeral" *The Fiddlehead*
"East of the Sun, West of the Moon" *The Fictional Café*
"The Fashionable Consumer to his Stove" *The Real Paper*
"The House of Old Lovers" *Gargoyle*
"How John Dean Got Drunk Every Night" *Invisible City*
"Murder at Harvard" *Borderlands: Texas Poetry Review*
"Spring Mourner" *Blue Buildings*
"Waking from a Nightmare" *The Fictional Café*
"The Would-Be Frog Wife" *Blue Unicorn*

To the many people in my life who have helped me in countless ways, my undying gratitude. I could never have done it without you.
And with special thanks to Katie for the dotted quarter note.

Publisher: Leah Maines
Editor: Christen Kincaid
Cover Art: "Far Away" by Sarah Sutro © 1998, www.sarahsutro.com
Author Photo: Jean M. Wolfe
Cover Design: Elizabeth Maines McCleavy

Printed in the USA on acid-free paper.
Order online: www.finishinglinepress.com
      also available on amazon.com
      and from the author at paulabonnell.net

Author inquiries and mail orders:
Finishing Line Press
P. O. Box 1626
Georgetown, Kentucky 40324
U. S. A.

Contents

Orpheus 1

Bluebeard 2

The Would-Be Frog Wife 4

In Which Mama Bear Loses her Grip 5

Waking from a Nightmare 6

Hop o' my Thumb 7

The Ant's Love Song to the Grasshopper 8

Ancestral Memories 9

The House of Old Lovers 10

Mithridates 11

What the Sirens Sang 12

Chinoiserie, Before the Wars 13

Civil War Funeral: The Soldier Speaks 15

Death Speeds Up 16

Murder at Harvard: Perpetual Motion Machine ... 17

How John Dean Got Drunk Every Night 19

The Fashionable Consumer to his Stove 20

Spring Mourner 21

East of the Sun, West of the Moon 22

On Looking at a Folio Score of Phædra
   in the Lower Depths of the Library 23

When is a door not a door?

when it's ajar

Orpheus

It was cold. I felt my way, following
drips of water down. It was dark.
Nothing I had ever done before
mattered like this; I stank of sweat
knowing the danger, the darkness, the captors—
but I found my voice—my need and
my power poured out together. The notes—
spiraling out in a green yearning
toward the light—flowered with her name.
Warmth, her familiar warmth moving
behind me, I clambered up to
the cave mouth and its scalding star.
I was hot and happy—I turned to tell her
"Wake up, wake up, it's only a dream!"

Bluebeard

i

I have seen them so many times,
lollygagging, wan in their chairs, their arms
slopped forward over the table.
After the jilting, stopped in mid-sentence,
agog at how you do, how you do not
care. Right where you abandoned them;
they are ashen in their chairs.
Silence compels me, what recognitions in slurs!
Each day they are different:
now gossiping, now seemly; now smelly,
now stoppered with cobwebs; today, bejewelled with gore.
The floor is littered with crystal drops—
what scutcheons of tears—
their faces plain as fear, all of our mouths asunder.

ii

The key gleams in the darkness.
It is a doorway to sadness; I have confused it
with myself. I long for its metal in my mouth;
I will tongue the keyhole with its answers,
know why curtains fling themselves into the hall.
I fit myself to the window
the way your tempers fitted my fears, your whispers my lust.
Now you fill me with urgent wetness
as the blood goes in a rush toward the wound
as the skin wizens along the scar.
Do not stop me with your silent stymies!
I will be through that open keyhole in a rush—
You are thrusting straight into my heart
with your silence pushing your refusal to be rushed.

The Would-Be Frog Wife

I am green and stout like you.
Your evening croakings
float me the way the lilies
hold us above the water.
I am rocking and rocking,
cradled on evenings of frog voice,
your burrings endless as nights are,
my listening like them, a home.

Your song says comforts
but it has other whispers too:
Princess, it says, and *kiss, throne, crown*.
I know *kiss*, but what are the others?
You say them over and over;
clicks and sibilants lift in your voice
the way our bubbles rise through the water.

What opens on the surface
is the air: this is the frog wife's song:
it is ourselves who
swim here in the pond.
When I lean over the lily pad's edge,
we are the ones who look back
out of the shine of the changeable water.
Evenings I gaze at the shapes that it offers.

If only I could lure you as I long to do
toward that edge of greenness—
yes, even if it upended,
spilling your rhymes in the water.
Frog, frog, sing "you dance, me dance!"
I would *kiss* you here in the flush of sunset,
frog as you are, frog, frog, frog.

In Which Mama Bear Loses her Grip

Details tell.
Loudmouth as a price tag
this on the pillow.
I know a bear hair
when I see one—
mine are as gruff and stiff as yours.
This undulant gold
is something else—
someone else.
Did you tuck her away
in our baby's bed?
Was she your baby first, here?

No, no, surely I've not got the story straight.
Some things are random.
Goldilocks, for instance,
innocent wanderer, fled from our room
alarmed by the hint of your musk.

Waking from a Nightmare

I am awash in the terrible seas of the night;
dream waves lift me and drop me.
Every hollow is a deep pit:
water for drowning is its floor
and I am sure to go under.
Gold could be lead in this lack of light,
and the sea so big
no one could measure its changes.

I am rising through blacknesses,
drowned in the bleak shutting out of
even the sheer blasts of the weather.
And as I am rising, utterly lost,
the dark water leaching my last warmth

you are there soft in the bed beside me,
the mercy of your flesh draped
exactly on your skeleton.

Your body posits axioms of warmth
as you draw breath, confident
as the geometer in the sand,
and though the soldier strike you
spilling your life force,
yours is the lever that could
move the earth.

Hop o' my Thumb

I dream of a man small as myself,
hands and feet like mine, legs bowed.
He has green eyes, he has a deep voice.
I will force him to come and live with me,
like a doll husband, mend my house.
He will skitter in and out the keyhole,
he will stay home days, trap the mouse.

It will be all play—
we'll grow children from the maple wings.
I will provide: money, laundry, meals.

At night we crawl in and out of
each other. In my excitement
I become enormous, a huge enfolding softness.

By morning he is big as a tree
and I nestle in his crooks,
before I scuttle out the door
with hairpins in my mouth.
I watch from across the street;
he is on the porch in his carpenter's apron,
pockets full of nails.

I am waiting for it
to whisper through him,
sweet recurrence
of his rare white disease.
In years to come
I will tell the children,
"He was green and strong."

The Ant's Love Song to the Grasshopper

What will my love do in the winter chill?
My worries ask; I fret about the frost.
This perfect green will hardly last through fall.

I search the chaff and fumble as I cull;
I turn each bit lest any good be lost.
What will my love do in the winter chill?

This summer singing quavers as it thrills—
Your flights begin to falter in the grass.
This perfect green will hardly last through fall.

If I begin to burrow while you loll
and still continue nibbling while you fast,
what will our love do in the winter chill?

Should I sprout wings and let my greenness sail
then, greensick, wait till slow ant thoughts can grasp
that perfect green would surely outlast fall?

Oh careless love, I quiver at your call
but sadly lisp my song in August dust:
What will my love do in the winter chill?
This perfect green will never last the fall.

Ancestral Memories

Chicken Little was right to be nervous.
As these large shadows swoop over me
my bird brain pronounces them hawks.
Then peeling paint hits the floor.
Horses shy at shadows the same way.
Their ancestral memories stir,
remembering when they were prey.
Listen! The ceiling is falling
whispering as it flops down in the middle of the night.

Maybe there was no hail
when Chicken Little's forebear hens
were laying and dreaming of Chanticleers—
I trust some essence of her fears.
If I in my kitchen start at hawks of paint
thinking hurried thoughts of where to hide the children—
why shouldn't she flare her feathers and squawk?
It's the self she spreads out, enfolding the chicks
like the knitted chicken tea cozy
or my great-great-grandmother Catherine Rutledge
hiking the children off to church
under her cloak
hidden from her orangeman husband.

The House of Old Lovers

Now they are my housemates,
each in his own room,
all tucked away.
Under my attentive eye here they are:
lifelike, conversational,
like that in-group, my old doll collection.
Do they twitch? Are they quelled?
They look at me head on,
they never hood their eyes—I see
small gleams come and go.
When I tamed them
and made them acquainted
one with another,
I barely knew what I was doing.
And now they are all here
mutely sleeping without me,
sucking their thumbs,
taking turns having me cut their hair.
All of us eat at the same table. Afterward
I just let them sit out on the porch
where they talk of hardware
and how to do this and that.
They fool themselves into thinking that later
they'll all compare notes. They never
do. I watch them through the
dining room window the way
a well-fed cat watches a
slow-moving lizard. None of them
sees my trick that keeps them all here
swilling the mash
and coming when I appear.
I whisper to them, "I am Circe"
but they hear nothing as they snuffle,
as they wheeze, as they grunt.
I go back to the kitchen and masturbate
at the thought of them milling around me,
their bristles bumping the backs of my legs.

Mithridates

You are wrong to call my feat perverse.
It seems so to you, no doubt,
but listen to what I've learned (and this is just a sample):
Faith and doubt are names for the same thing,
white names for the weather that blows green and dark,
halves of one another, you-and-I opposites—
like mirrored ringing, reflected echoing, reader
and writer, understanding, knowing
(arrival through) each other.
I have gone far from where I began
(emerging, becoming, moving) to know what
came before (meeting, blind, possible)
(the pair and the child with the same origin)
to come to this place which is none—
this opposition of sames, conjunction of opposites,
this jangle of now where the future
used to be, the past not to be.
Well may you ask of what use
is the strength I've acquired: power to withstand
pain seeming only to invite more,
way of wanting what's lost. Listen!
I can almost let you in on the secret
here in the gasp before death: I live, I breathe.

What the Sirens Sang

To every man a different song.
The song of desire for knowledge of him,
the song asking that he unfold, disclose,
the song claiming him: I know you through
and through, the song that saw and touched
what hurt, the song that knew.
For the sirens were women of great learning
and from the smell of a man's body
blown to them on the wind as
his ship passed through their ken,
his smell compound of salt and sweet,
of keen and dark, obscure and plain,
the smell of a being with only one mouth,
they could discern, could make a brew of simples
to bring him sleep, and sweet awakening in their arms.
They took him then, laved him,
shared him among themselves
and sent him back to a world of men
from a world of women with sharp noses
and soft mouths. He remembered always
their hands giving him ease,
their hair falling to touch his face,
and their voices, the voices of women
who wanted to know, who knew.

Chinoiserie, Before the Wars

Brighton, Sussex

Only a sun-mad prince could ask
bamboo shapes to be carved from English beech.
The prince's balustrades are all chinoise,
insouciant shapes which make up rails
astride the inner edge of stairs which lead
to upper floors which hang beneath
the roof's mélange of onion domes and minarets.

The crowd allowed into the corridor
is stepping out of step: its walking sets anod
the yellow heads of wood nabobs.
And in the South Room, Nelson's gilded-dolphin furniture
elicits *ahs*. But no one sees
the mantel timepiece where by writhing waves
a golden Triton blows his wreathèd horn.

Milton, Massachusetts

A four-square Yankee mansion; in the yard
fu lions and a sign, "Museum
of the China Trade." Rich cargo
is inside: what China made
when Boston asked: inlays, hand-painted
wallpaper, a desk of dull-red gloss
with secret drawers, a dragon
rug with cloud-and-mountain edge.

And in a glass-front case, one dinner plate,
one from a full set of twelve.
On it in blue and red, a bridge, a stream,
and poised above the blue arch of the bridge,
in crisp blue letters: *GREEN*
with a red arrow pointing down.

Civil War Funeral:
The Soldier Speaks

Dusty broodings of a velvet quilt
in wine and flesh, maroon and brown
shrouding me, now nubbed and purpled . . . still . . .
but then—by tongues and fingers wound,
turned and twisted, talked to life.
                                   In yards
of cambric by wells of tea, noise fades.
Tired, bent, a soldier from afar
comes, says that I am dead.
                                They made,
bright with sorrow, Joseph's colored coat.
Their dusty sobs sift through my throat.

Death Speeds Up

pulls in to the curb
steps out of the dream car
ambles into the house
settles down in the spare room
leaves notes by the sink

he'll want the other twin next
then crawl into mine
forcing himself into me
finally stuffing me down

Murder at Harvard:
Perpetual Motion Machine

Dr. Parkman, how your bones do knock about!

I gave that old buzzard a turkey
but he tricked me, he unbricked you;
you steel-tooth codger, you cadger.

(My face floats above the fiery bowl.)

Parkman, I have you in my power.
No more of your glints at my lectures,
your outthrust chin,
your rudeness thrust at my rambles,
your taunts.

It used to be
you were creditor, I debtor.
Now I'm uncreator; you're just dead.
Harsh reversal, eh?
How does it feel?
or can't you tell?
Can you no longer tell how anything feels?
Is that why you knock about so?

So what if I've gone from doctor to sawbones?

Don't you feel how I am
quieting the violence of your demands
with these streamers of water,
playing out your colors like
New Year's streamers left out in the rain?

Chemicals to chemicals,
sums to naught.
Well, Parkman, there you are

So what is that damned clanking in the pipes?
I could swear it was you,
rattling my cage again.

What a talker, even as a corpse,
what a clerk's way with figures,
what a counter, what a clocker,
But after all, Parkman,
what a dead issue.

How John Dean Got Drunk Every Night

1.   The lifting of the glass
2. a) The bite of the proof
or b) The glugging of beer

3.   The flattening of the accents of the
voices which never stop repeating
accuser to conscience
C to A
Q to A, A to Z
Pudding, Alice
Alice, pudding

4.   Tell all
to nothingness do sink

5.   The scenes so vivid
removed to the drunken distance
properly brutal, properly loutish
with the right proper morals tagged on
but all this having nothing to do with
myself

6.   I can only renounce
power for power

7.   I will write a book.

The Fashionable Consumer to his Stove

Come live with me and be my stove
and we will all the pleasures prove
that dampers, flues, and hods I wield,
woods and steepy downdrafts yield.

And logs will sit o'er fire bricks
freeing the photosynthetic fix
by lengthy flame paths to whose calls
the kettle sings its madrigals.

And I will make thy fuelbed airy
with drafts both main and secondary.
I'll bring a hearth rug and a kitten
to purr beside your smooth black satin;

a baffle of a fireproof board
that you for us may make untoward
fur-linèd slippers for the cold;
and we may keep our bucks and gold.

A lid of steel, a rake, and poker,
and I will be thy faithful stoker.
And if these pleasures may thee move,
come live with me and be my stove.

The BTUs shall dance and sing
with thee alight each Jan. evening.
If these delights thy currents move,
then live with me and be my stove.

Spring Mourner
homage to Sylvia Plath, 1932-1963

i

Rosary gabble niggles at you.
You answer idiotically:
 Go be wan, woebegone.

You reek of glamor,
turn your back on the
deep-interred
black-glimmering casque.

You whisper moronically:
 Give me my mirror.
 The iris has a fat lip.
 The smoke twirls like a feather boa.

Weedy intruder,
your blacks iridesce,
generous as coalflowers.

ii

Glabrous mushrooms rise slope-shouldered
through snippets of grass.
You are tuberous;
you hunch,
growth without light
your only thought.

Evenings gape before you
as you fret for shorter nights
and mornings when you will
open pallid as a paper blossom
out of opal sleep.

East of the Sun, West of the Moon

In the west, the sun is setting
In the east, the moon is rising
Two celestial lamps, the wayfarer in between
It is still day, soon to be dark

The quest fits the soul
as the bear's skin the bear—
it is loose, mobile, sliding around
the body it encloses;
it suits the need for escape.

The raven lands in the snow
This is no time for doubt
but the horizon offers no guidance
as it rings the place where
the wayfarer stands

The moon's light is damped by a cloud
The shadow of a speck in the distance
darkens and lengthens till the shape
of a roof is drawn on the snow

A word hangs in the frozen air: *Morfedloch*
The traveler turns toward
the distant hut. The bird
lifts awkwardly into the air, flapping
and clocking its thick call.

**On Looking at a Folio Score of *Phædra*
in the Lower Depths of the Library**

Benjamin Britten interspersed his Italian
with English, telling his mezzo (Janet Baker)
when to be *Broadly flowing*,
his percussionists when to perform
in (*agitated crochets*),
and I read his parentheses as
part of the instruction, too.

      Y'know? I'd like to try
to hit those notes myself
in parenthetical agitated crochets.

How specifically he imagined the performance
as he called it into being on the page,
transcribing everything his pen could label
with words or punctuation in any
of his natural languages

After the part where he wrote
pizz. *arco V pizz.* (*with tutti; arco*),
he asked the coming music
to be *Fast and impulsive* (♩. = 126) *attaca*
He directed that section 8 be delivered
ironically (*non dim.*) with section 9
as before.
      On the page, these sections are
prefaced by their numbers, and
as the score is handwritten, not printed,
instead of such typographic alerts as italic
or boldface, Britten draws a square
to surround each presiding number.
      To me
following this score, not able
to read music well enough
to hear it in my head as

I page through it, it feels as though I
am walking through a city of
his imagination and these are
the leafy squares where streets
pause in their relentless gridding
of the map; the "squared" numbers
seeming to name parts of
the city, adjoining neighborhoods.

Each square leads to another section.

With square 17 begin
Slow minims—from Square 23 on
is to be *Lively*—and what a help to know
these things if you were Janet Baker
or the percussionist facing an assembly
of striking and strikeable objects
to know <u>how</u> you were to be going,
going as you moved along, along to where
the characters and audience
began to understand they would
go

In square 23 where it was *Lively*
you would also be working *Very broadly*
and he told you so when it
was to be (*soft sticks*)
(How natural for those to be
parenthetically soft sticks.)
                                      Square 26—
with *ADAGIO* in large block capitals—
is also *a tempo, quietly*
                                  (By now you, too,
the reader, understand this
Italianate English, or anglo-

coupled Italian as all one tongue, the speech
of music, asking everything,
everything . . .)

In square 29, Baker will
sing *Very soft and free*
and when she comes to
her final phrase—her words all
written by Robert Lowell in
his best English equivalent
of Racine's French and
selected by Britten from
the whole of what Lowell
wrote to yield the relatively
few words which this score
renders in music—her last
words are "dying away" sung > *ppp*.
Beneath them Britten
has written *quick (as before)*
and also suggests to the musicians
The rest, muted

While a practicing lawyer, **Paula Bonnell** began publishing her poems in such places as *Southern Poetry Review*, *Manhattan Poetry Review*, and *Rattle*. Her first collection, *Message*, includes "Eurydice," a sequence chosen by Albert Goldbarth for a *Poet Lore* narrative-poetry award, and "Midwest," broadcast on *The Writer's Almanac*. Her *Airs & Voices* was selected by poet and critic Mark Jarman for the Ciardi Prize and published by BkMk Press, a university-affiliated publisher at the University of Missouri-Kansas City, with quotes from Richard Wilbur, Maxine Kumin, and X. J. Kennedy. Meanwhile she discontinued the practice of law, and now works primarily as a writer. Her chapbook *Before the Alphabet* is a story in free verse of a child's kindergarten year, with quotes from Megan Marshall, Nick Samaras, and Leah Maines.

Bonnell's essays and book reviews have appeared in *The Philadelphia Inquirer*, *The Christian Science Monitor*, *Boston Review*, and *The New York Times Book Review*, among others. Individual poems by Bonnell have received awards in competitions sponsored by the literary magazines *Negative Capability* and *Kalliope* as well as the Chester H. Jones Foundation, and her fiction has been recognized by an award from the NEA/PEN Syndicated Fiction project and publication in the *Kansas City Star Sunday Magazine* and the *Chapel Hill Village Advocate*. She is a PEN New England Discovery writer.

Since 2007, poems by Bonnell have been published by a variety of print and online journals including *The American Poetry Review*, *Gargoyle*, *The Hopkins Review*, *The Hudson Review*, *Oberon*, *Rattle*, and *Spillway*. Sequences of her poems have also appeared: "Canoe Trip" in *The Poetry Porch*, and "A Spy at Large in the Printed Matter" in *Slippery Elm Literary Journal*, as well as a six-poem feature in *The Fictional Café*. Links to those available free online can be found at www.paulabonnell.net. Also some poems and her essay "The Poetry of Wisława Szymborska" are at the website.

www.ingramcontent.com/pod-product-compliance
Lightning Source LLC
LaVergne TN
LVHW050046090426
835510LV00043B/3328